ScottForesman
Balloons
1

Authors

Mario Herrera

Barbara Hojel

D1277975

 LONGMAN

Addison Wesley Longman

New York • London • Hong Kong

Reviewers/Consultants

Marilyn Moyer
Instituto de Desarrollo Infantil
  de Puebla, Educando
Puebla, Mexico

Jeane Jacobs
Instituto Mexicano Madero
Puebla, Mexico

Lucila Sotomayor de Gil
Instituto D'Amicis
Puebla, Mexico

Rebeka Dyer Ortega
Colegio Las Hayas
Jalapa, Mexico

Angélica Arreola
El Principito de Izcantla and
  Colegio Yoliztli
Cholula, Mexico

Rosi Rosete
Anglo-Mexicano Institute
Instituto Juárez Lincoln
Puebla, Mexico

Susan Grim
Instituto Juárez Lincoln
Puebla, Mexico

Margarita Matte
Guadalajara, Mexico

Angelina Del Campo
Proulex
Guadalajara, Mexico

Laura Afif de Trabolsi
Georgina Muñoz de Elizarraras
Instituto Irlandes
Mexico City, Mexico

María Eugenia Carballo
Virginia Hernández
Instituto Técnico y Cultural
Mexico City, Mexico

Thelma Péres
Casa Thomas Jefferson
Brasilia, Brazil

Alice de Fajardo
Newman School
Santa fe de Bogota, Colombia

José Pablo (Pepito) Sánchez
  Cartolín
Lima, Peru

Giovanna Nicoletti
Americano Miraflores
Lima, Peru

Patricia Vásquez
Abraham Lincoln Cooperative
  School
Lima, Peru

Linda Amin
KFUPM Kindergarten
Dhahran, Saudi Arabia

Kemale Pinar
Al-Faisaliah Girls' School
Al-Khobar, Saudi Arabia

Robin de Andrés
Colegio Ecole International
  Section
Asturias, Spain

Stuart Bowie
Akiko Saito
Tokyu Seminar BE
Tokyo, Japan

Julie Gienger
Yokohama YMCA
Yokohama, Japan

Masumi Ide
AXIS Language Institute
Tokyo, Japan

Yuko Kikuchi
Tokyo YWCA
Tokyo, Japan

Emiko Suzuka
St. Dominic Gakuen
Tokyo, Japan

Reiko Tada
Global English House
Nishinomiya, Japan

Sarah Jang
Neo English Academy
Seoul, South Korea

Tim Budden
ELSI Taiwan
Taipei, Taiwan

Lional Lan
Jorden Language School
Taipei, Taiwan

Peggy Huang
The Joy Children's Language
  School
Taipei, Taiwan

Shu-yi Lin
The Joy Children's Language
  School
Taipei, Taiwan

Cindy Yi
Caves Ltd.
Taipei, Taiwan

Balloons
Level 1 Student Book

Addison Wesley Longman, 10 Bank Street, White Plains, NY 10606

Executive editor: Anne Stribling
Development editor: Yoko Mia Hirano
Director of design and production: Rhea Banker
Production editor: Liza Pleva
Cover design: Rhea Banker
Manufacturing supervisor: Edie Pullman
Color separator: TSI Graphics
Text design: MKR
Text composition: MKR

Illustrations:
Bernard Adnet 41, 83-84; Yvette Banek 20-21, 30-31; Shirley Beckes 60-61; Lisa Berrett 46-47; Paige Billin-Frye 17, 79-80; Susan Calitri 4-5, 36-37, 75-76; Shelley Deitrich 9; Suzanne DeMarco 68-69; Jill Dubin 14-15, 77-78; Nate Evans 65; Ruth Flanigan 12-13, 49, 54-55, 85-86; Steve Henry 28-29, 52-53, 87-88; Joan Holub 2-3, 10-11, 18-19, 26-27, 34-35, 42-43, 50-51,58-59, 66-67; Ben Mahan 6-7; Kimble Mead 22-23, 25; Daphne McCormack 44-45; Cary Pillo 70-71, 91-92; Steve Sullivan 73; Rebecca Thornburgh 33, 81-82; George Ulrich 38-39; Gregg Valley 57; Bari Weismann 62-63, 89-90

Balloon Art: MKR Electronic File
Mascot Art: Karen Lee Schmidt
Picture Dictionary: Rita Lascaro
Cover Photography: Richard Hutchings

ISBN: 0-201-35119-6
  3 4 5 6 7 8 9 10–PO–02 01 00 99 98

ScottForesman

Balloons

1

Contents

1

My Classroom

Unit 1 My School Warm Up

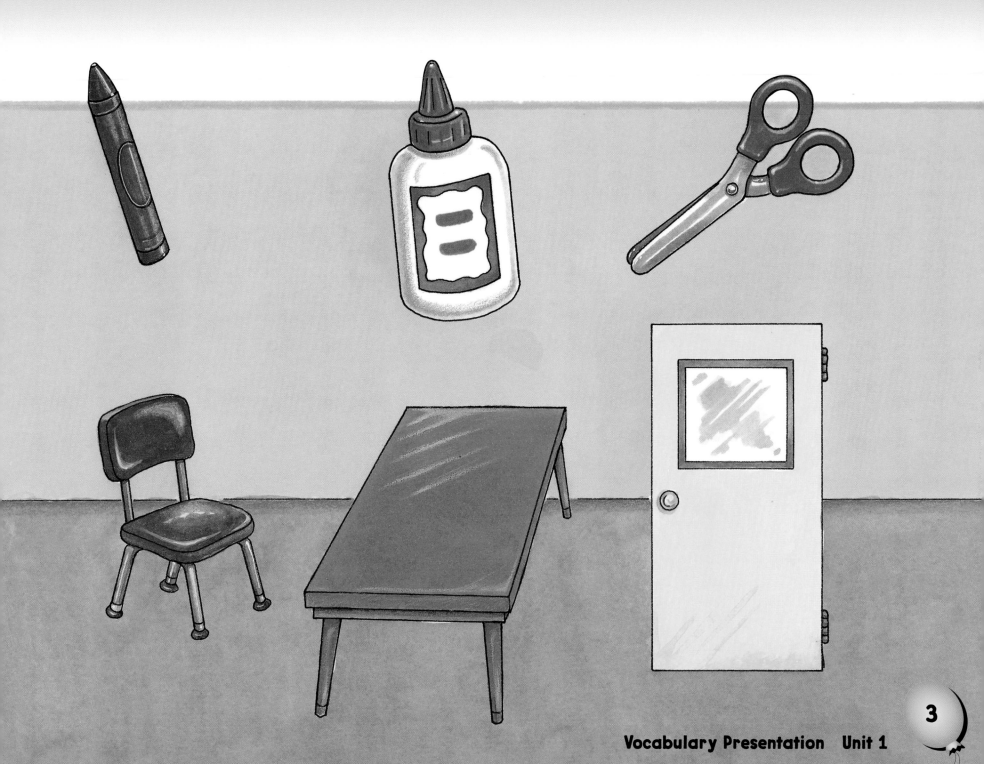

Vocabulary Presentation   Unit 1

Unit 1　Shapes: circle

Draw Circles   Unit 1

5

 6

Unit 1　Colors: red, blue

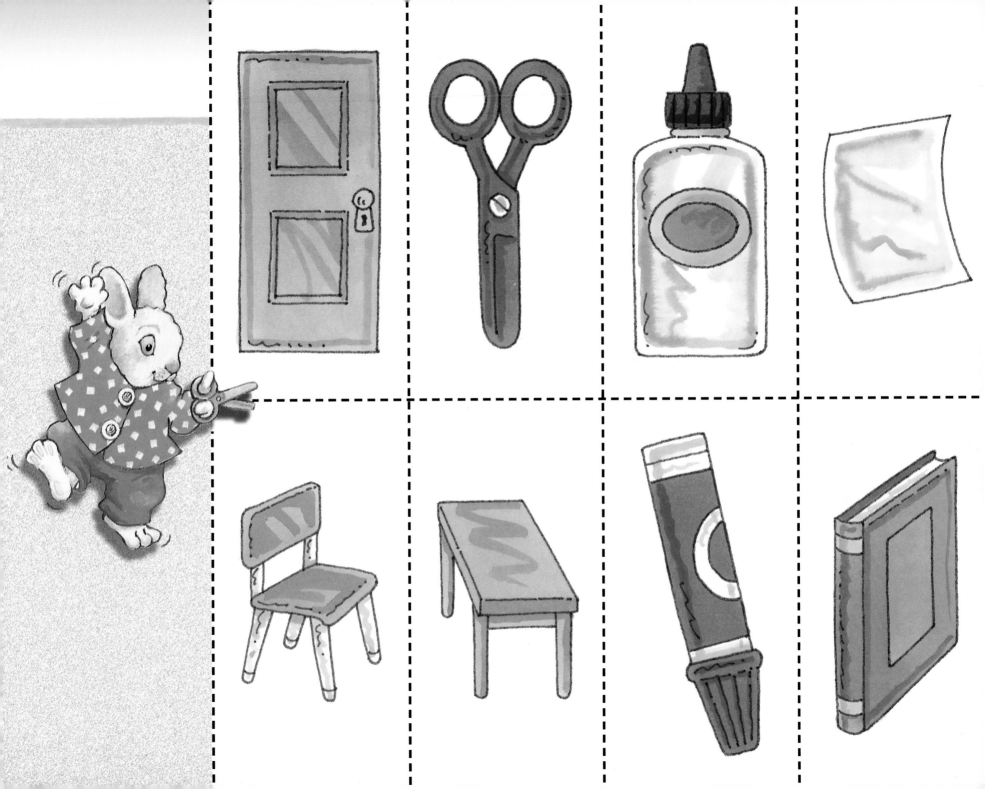

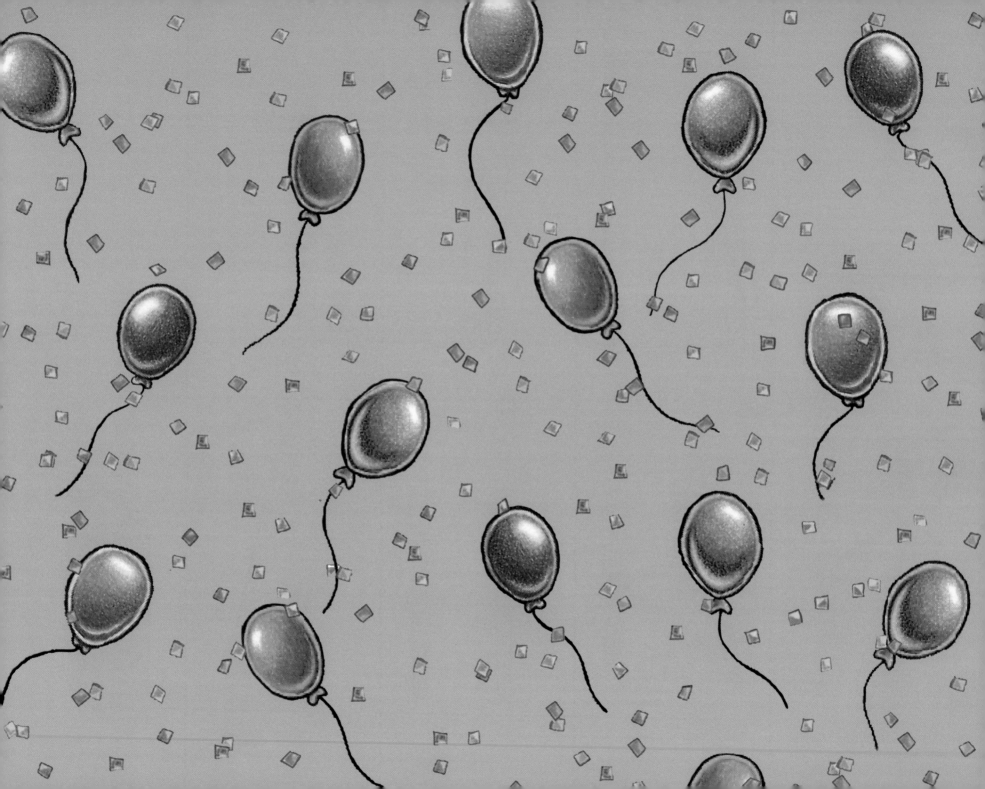

Here I Am!

Vocabulary Presentation   Unit 2

Unit 2 Count: 1-2; Colors: yellow, green

Unit 2   Parts of the Body

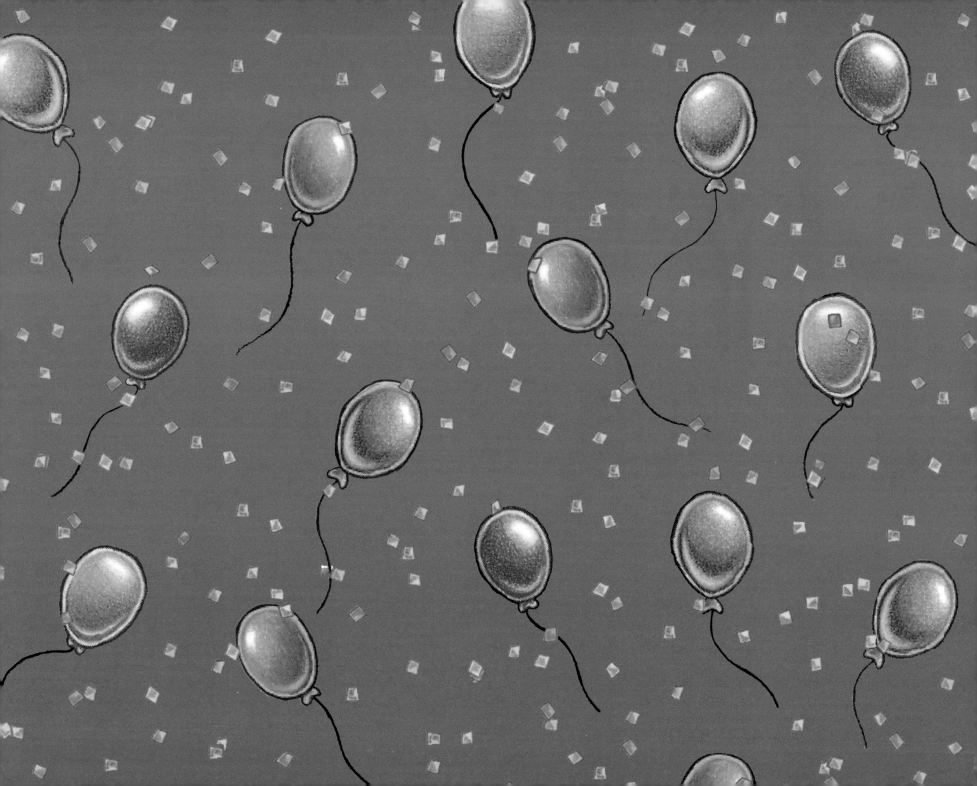

Our Families

20

Unit 3   Places We Go; Colors: purple, orange

Draw a Family   Unit 3

22

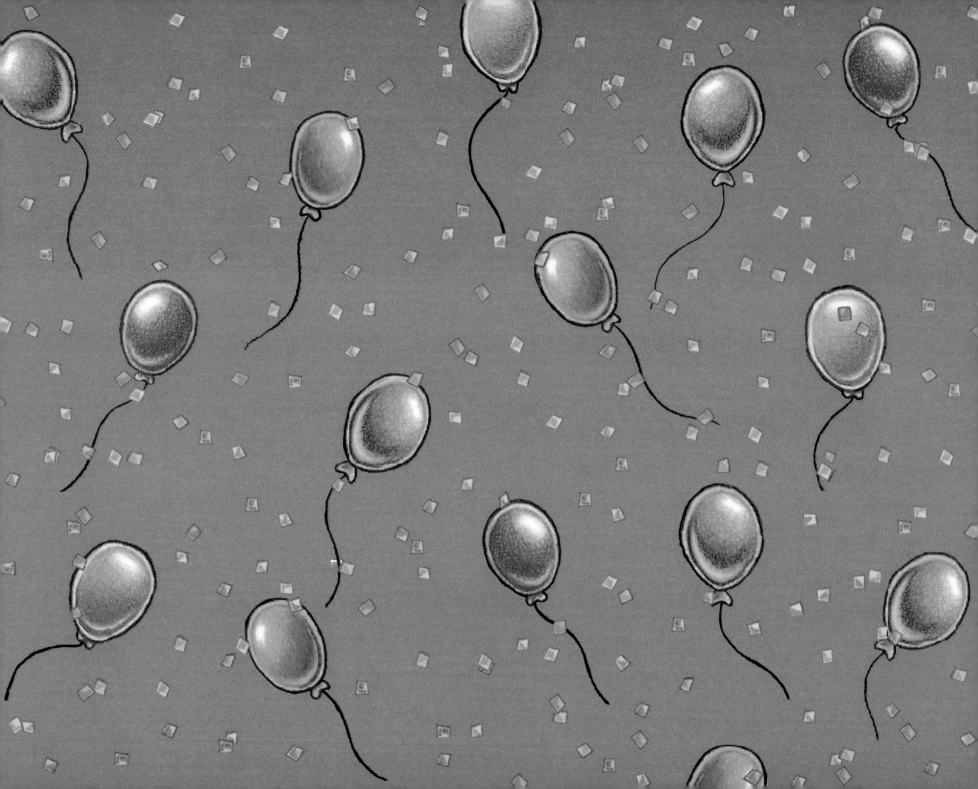

Animals Around Us

27

Vocabulary Presentation   Unit 4

Unit 4 Prepositions: over, under

29

Draw a Favorite Pet   Unit 4

Unit 4   Prepositions: in, on; Count: 1–4

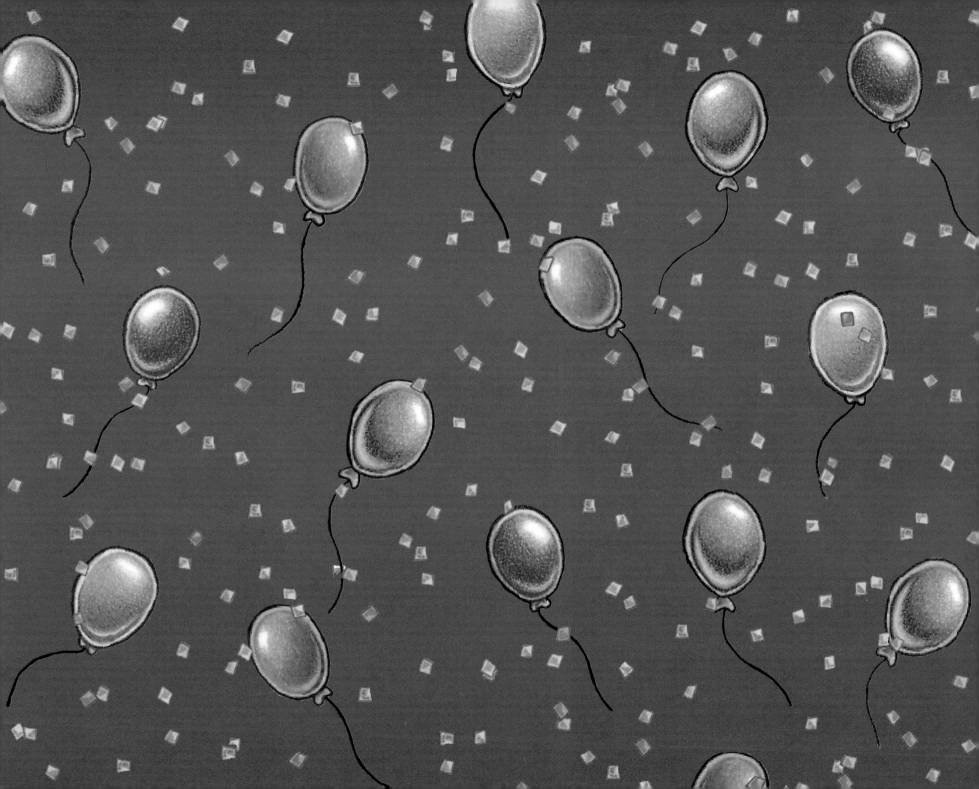

Everyday Clothes

Unit 5   Things We Wear   Warm Up

Vocabulary Presentation   Unit 5

Unit 5 Prepositions: in front of, behind, next to; Count: 1-5

Draw a Favorite Outfit   Unit 5

Unit 5   Shapes: triangle, circle, square; Colors: pink

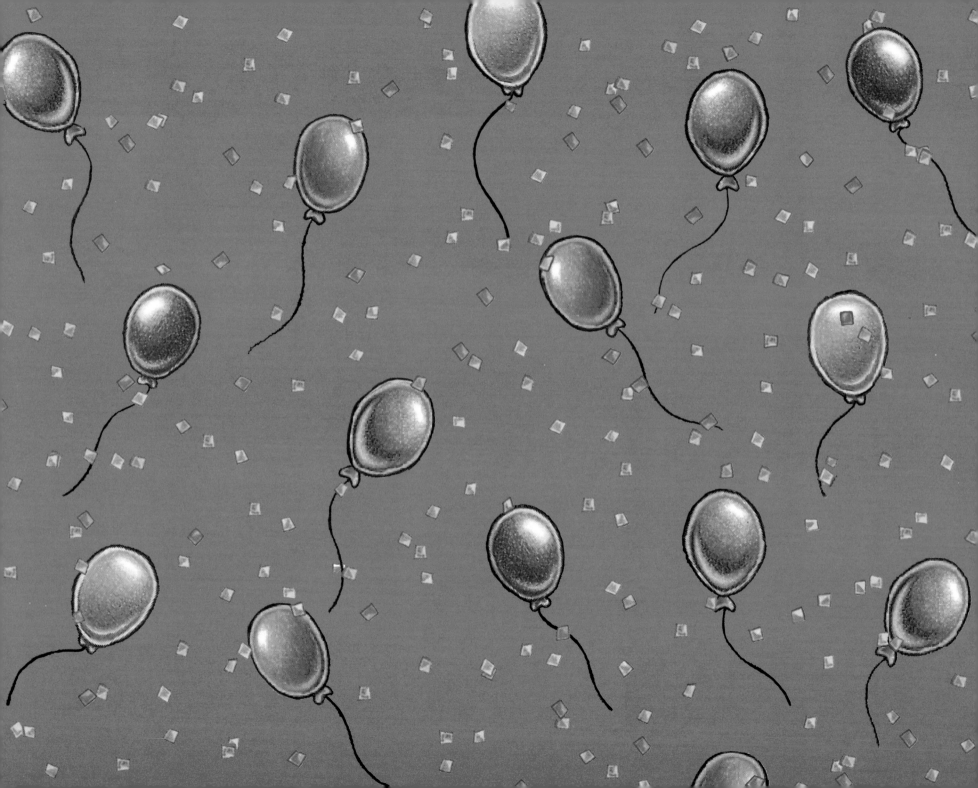

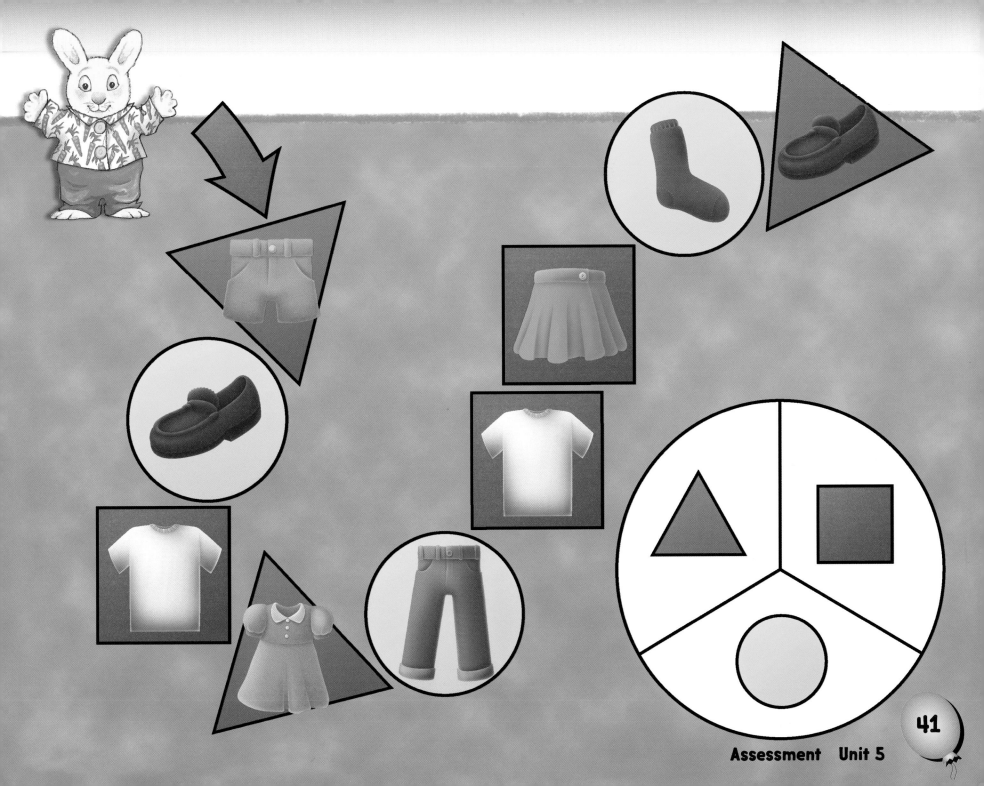

It's a Party!

Unit 6   Things We Eat   Warm Up

43

Unit 6 Foods We Like

46

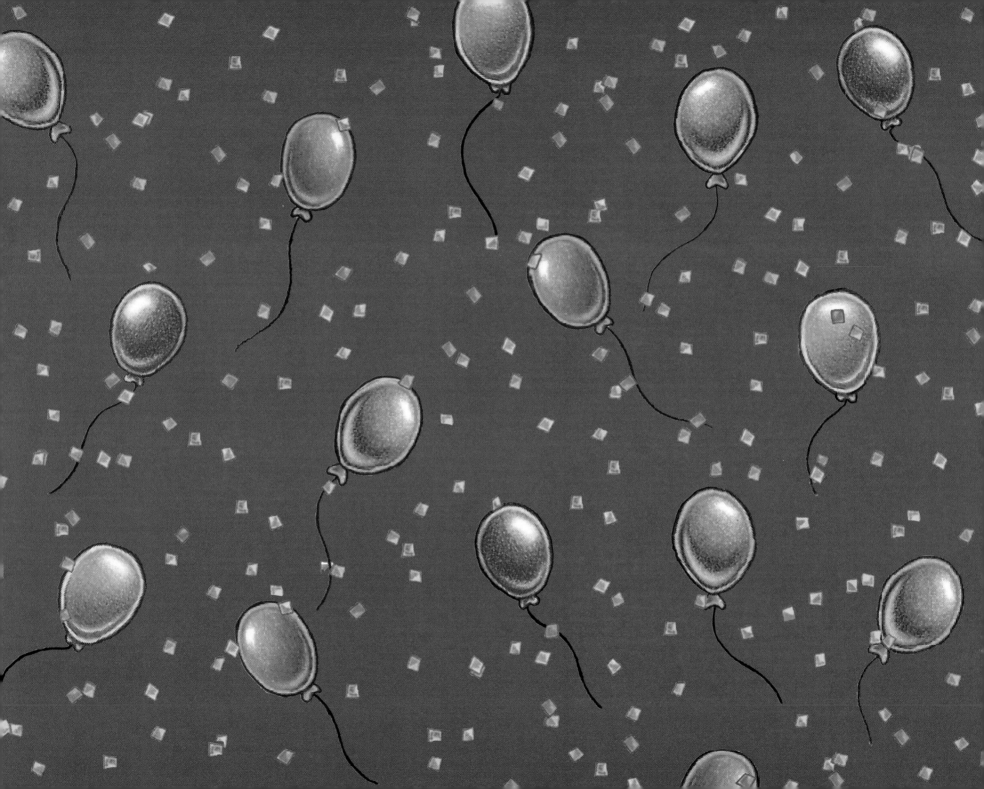

Around My Home

Unit 7   Count: 1-7; Prepositions: next to, in front of, on

Draw a Neighborhood   Unit 7

Unit 7 Action Words

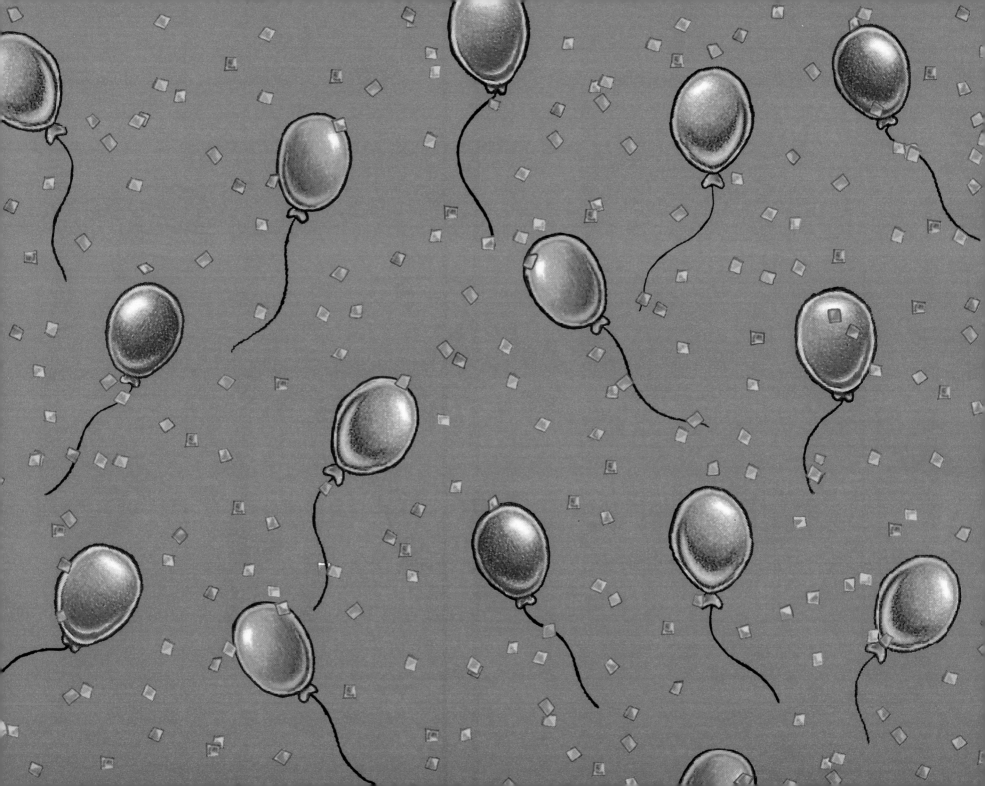

Cleaning Up!

Vocabulary Presentation   Unit 8

Unit 8   Sort Objects; Count: 1-8

Make Recycled Art   Unit 8

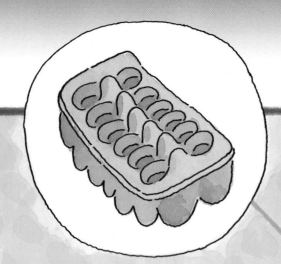

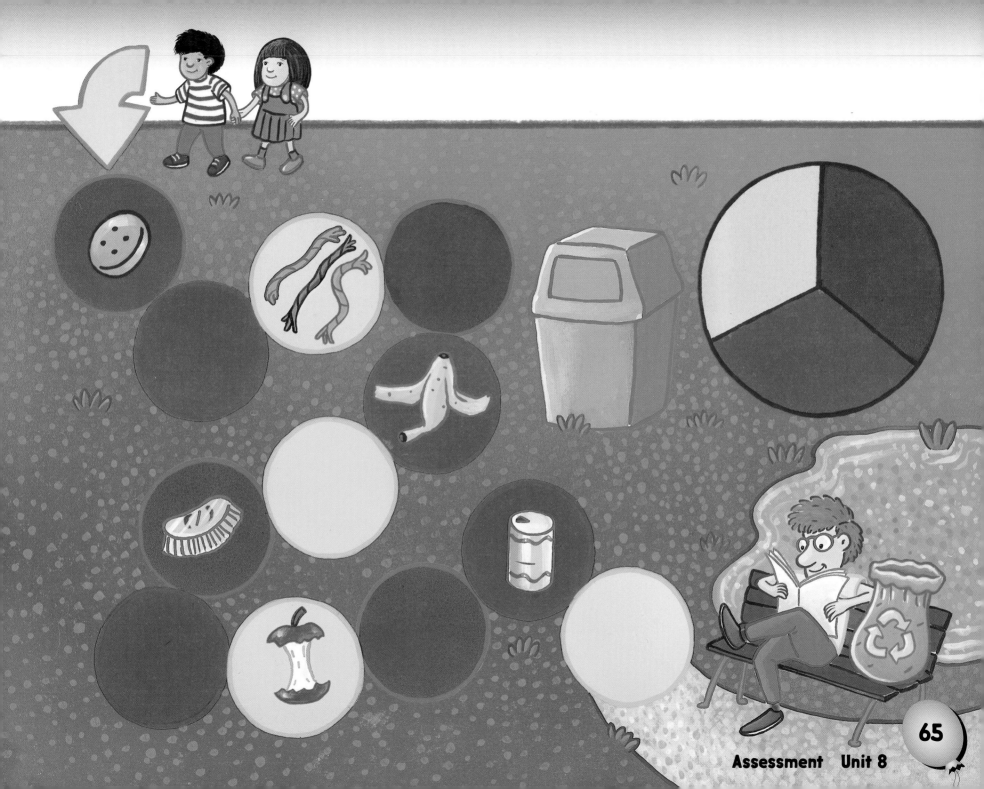

Growing Together!

Unit 9   Changes, Changes   Warm Up

67

Unit 9   Classify Objects

Draw Something That Grows   Unit 9

Unit 9   Sequence Events

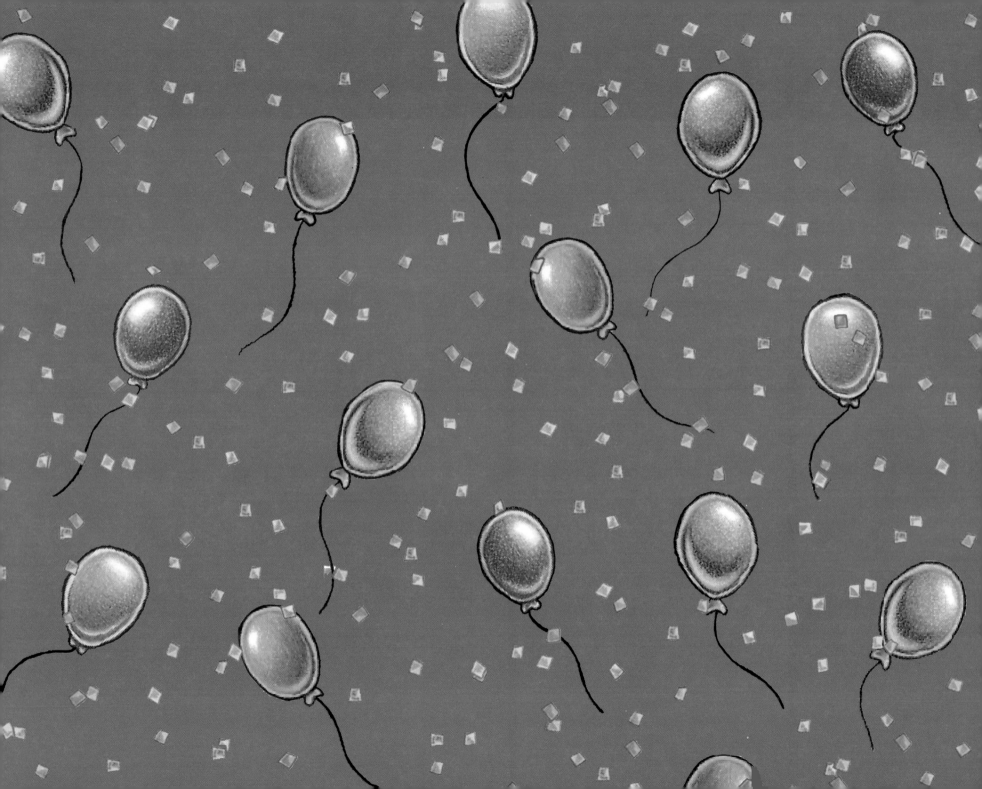

School Day

A Family Picnic

Dog at Play

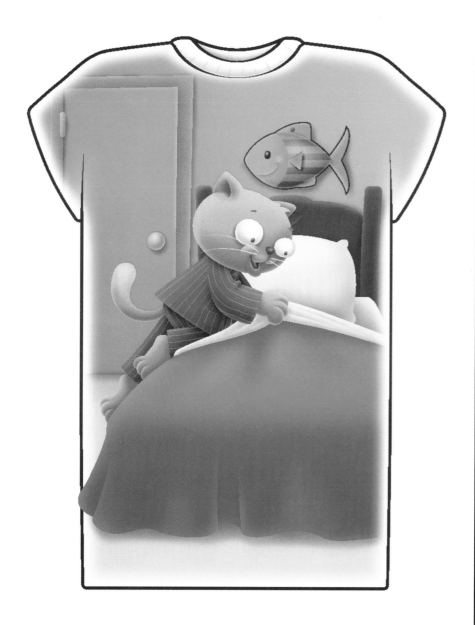

Cat's Clothes

Play Day